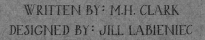

love who YOU ARE

WRITTEN BY: M.H. CLARK
DESIGNED BY: JILL LABIENIEC

BEGIN BY
loving yourself.

LOVE YOURSELF FOR THE WAYS

you have grown.

LOVE

YOUR FIERCE INTELLIGENCE,
YOUR DEEP POTENTIAL.

LOVE

THE WAYS YOU ARE LIKE
NO ONE ELSE.

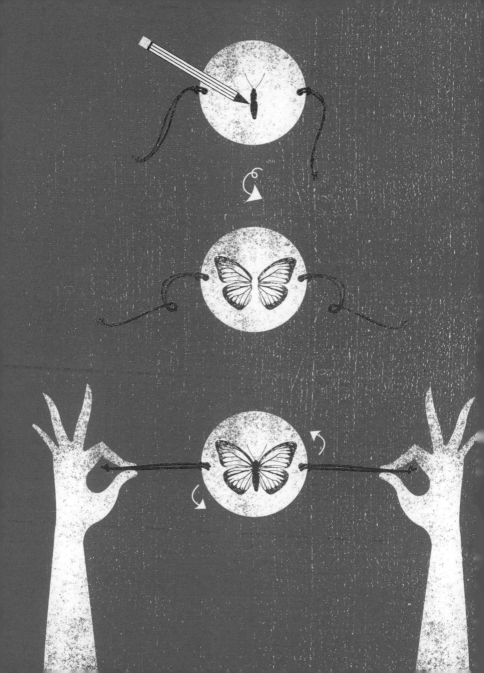

LOVE THE WAY YOU CHANGE YOUR MIND.
LOVE THE FACT THAT YOU ARE NOT
THE SAME PERSON YOU USED TO BE.
love the person you are becoming.

LOVE YOUR

future wild

MISTAKES.

LOVE
THE TOMORROWS YOU
ARE HEADING INTO.
LOVE
THAT YOU WILL END
UP DOING MORE THAN
YOU CAN IMAGINE.

LOVE IT
WHEN YOU'RE BOLD ENOUGH
TO STAND ALONE.
LOVE IT
WHEN YOU'RE TENDER ENOUGH
TO NEED SUPPORT.

LOVE YOUR UPS AND YOUR DOWNS,
your sudden cravings, your quirks,
YOUR HOPES FOR SOMETHING MORE.

LOVE THE PARTS OF YOU
that need more loving.

and always,

EVEN WHEN IT IS LOTS OF WORK,
LOVE THE PARTS OF YOU THAT YOU
WOULD PREFER TO HIDE.

ORGET THAT

are full of

POSSIBILITY.

do not forget that the whole world

AWAITS YOU.

YOU ARE RIGHT
where you belong.

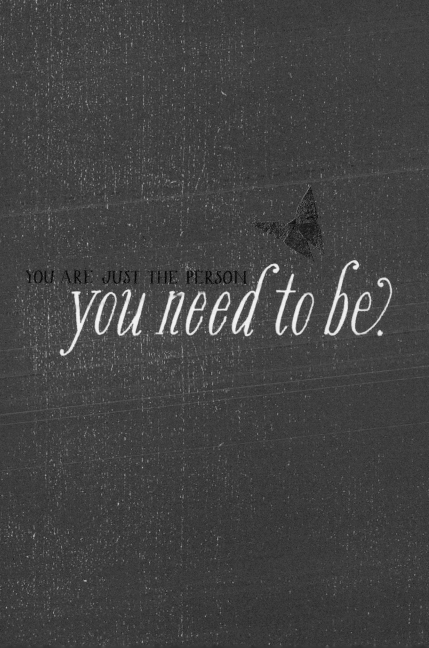

YOU ARE JUST THE PERSON
you need to be.

love yourself gently, with your whole

HEART.

love your silliness
AND
your seriousness.

LOVE
your complexities.

delight in the ways you cannot be

DEFINED

and love the ways you cannot be

TAMED.

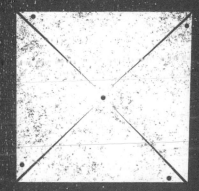

AND LOVE IT WHEN

that learning has been good.

LOVE YOURSELF
WHEN THINGS ARE HARD.
LOVE YOURSELF
EVEN WHEN IT HURTS.

love yourself

ENOUGH TO GIVE YOURSELF THE

THINGS YOU NEED.

and keep lov

THA

BECOME

ourself until

LOVE

HABIT.

LOVE YOURSELF

SO THAT THE WORLD CAN SEE

HOW BEAUTIFULLY

YOU DESERVE TO BE TREATED.

and KEEP ON LOVING YOURSELF
WITH JOY AND PERSEVERANCE.

RIGHT DOWN TO THE BOTTOM OF YOU, *as you love a dear friend.*

COMPENDIUM.
live inspired

WITH SPECIAL THANKS TO THE
ENTIRE COMPENDIUM FAMILY.

CREDITS:
Written by: M.H. Clark
Designed by: Jill Labieniec
Edited by: Amelia Riedler
Creative Direction by: Julie Flahiff

ISBN: 978-1-938298-06-6

6th printing. Printed in China with soy inks.